SHOOT OUT WITH THE CONSPIRACY

21ST CENTURY ERA

SANJIVNI SINHA

To everyone, who thinks.

Contents

Acknowledgements

To those who I love, and those who will be reading this book. You all, eventually will be part of this roller coaster saga, as you are going to put your time, and try to understand my story. You might enter my shoes, if scenario(s) relates to you, but trust me it is co-incident. To everyone, who no matter what, stood beside me, and became part of my life in some way.

: I Acknowledge

Preface

Shoot out with the conspiracy, an idea that got ideated, during the 2020 COVID pandemic, when the world came to pause, and gave time to work on something else, while working from home. The book came into existence ,when I just looked back at various life happenings, and wondered if everything was a conspiracy, rather than a natural event.

My intention, is not to challenge the obvious, but definitely, I sensed, a different kind of slavery, had rooted in the society, in the form of "hearing - hearing before acting, hearing before speaking, in a nutshell, hearing before anything". Everyone was following the same path, because everyone else was following, a way to be in a competition or in a rat race; else dictated to a level, where quitting, the only choice left.

It was not true for a society, or a country, or a continent; but apparently, everywhere same happenings were happening, which concreted the fact that "the people who are leading the world, are dictators. and that they are favoring certain people, or for that matter, a family",

The book walks through various happenings, of my life, from childhood confusion to vision blackness, when truth surfaced in front of me, and why I became a rebel in my youth, - to unwind the conspiracy, and understand who are leading the world. Similar to many, at some stage, the choice left with me, was to start hearing or choose death, but apparently social media acted as an elixir. to untangle the hidden motive, of plot. Let's start with childhood memories in Chapter 1.

Prologue

The book describes small things, which I guess everyone must have witnessed, but have ignored it. Something like getting ahead of competition, to get what one wants. It also tells, how at young age, all that mattered was fair skin, and education system needed, cent percent from students. It beautifully describes, the importance of reading beyond lines so, that one is confident that he/she understands, and went through everything before raising voice for justice.

Slowly, truth surfaced, when you are told be happy, with the title you received, and do not expect the prize, and one realizes, that education is not the real power. Multiple hats, is the key to success ,because you know everything, if you know the meaning of multiple hats. My journey, to find the true meaning, of everything, began with the word "Date".

Age is just a number, if true, then hopefully, society will not tag everything with age, and there will be more successful women, in the world, as it will give more freedom. The author, through the story, tries to explain, why people are killing their passion, as one who follows passion, would eventually be getting low paying job.

If, but, whatsoever, was a way to force oneself on another, in terms of making anyone to agree with disagree. Feedback, which meant for constructive criticism, somehow, constructive has got eliminated, and only criticism, has remained. One can chase anything, and do anything, but only if he/she is healthy. So, health is true wealth.

Furthermore, norm displacement has changed, the basics, which has challenged the ways, things are done. Lastly, the last challenge, was to trust Goddess and Gods, and do your best to free yourself, in every sense.

Foreword

The story, holds true for any student, who had chosen, to learn, over heraing to the power. If anyone, who had spoken only truth, had to face the power, as it shakes the core of people, who are leading the world. Life, itself is a lesson, but to change the world, a student needs to learn the rules, and play carefully against the players, and become a game changer, else fall into the trap like others and live life on their pieces.

: A Student

CHAPTER ONE

RAT RACE

While I was growing up, atleast till 4th grade, I had never cared about failures. All that mattered, was getting up every morning, looking forward to going to school, meeting friends, and in between learning basics of education.

It was an Indian education system, where I learned all subjects till school. My early education included Mathematics, English, Science, History, Geography, General Knowledge, Hindi, and German.

As far as I recalled, I changed my school, when I was in 8th Grade. I opted for one of the best schools in India, known for its quality education. The kindergarten, and primary school were fun, and I was among the top three students, always. Being among the top three signified, excelling in education, sports, and extra curriculum activities.

But, as I changed schools, I realized the competition the world had. As I estimated the number of youths in school, and extrapolated the competition in the world, it fractured my ego. It was a hard hit, not seeing myself, in the top three, for that matter, not even in the top 10. It was the time, when I understood; anything was possible.

"One can be at the zenith, with a belief, no one can beat, but the next moment, one realizes, many are ahead of you".

At that time, I became part of the rat race. Competition became life, friends were competitors, and other adjectives like:

"Hate, dislike, jealousy, anger, greed, and other negative ones", enhanced not only my vocabulary, but defined me.

I missed my old school, but that was replaced by, "I want to be, ahead of the competition, or get into the top medical college, and other rat race phenomenon". Though it happened from 8th grade, but it killed the healthy competition spirit, and ignited aggressive competition spirit, or the saying,

"Everything is fare in love and war".

The saying was very much true, as everyone dispensed the same vibes, of being ahead of the competition at any cost, the only way to get what one wanted.

CHAPTER TWO

BE YOURSELF

But not getting what I wanted, at that time, also taught me, to be happy, with what I had. School days, were still those days, which were like a shell, protected from all sides. I realized, if I focused on other individuals' achievements, I would be unhappy, and constantly overthinking. I shifted my focus, from-around competition-to-competition-with myself. But one fact, that I am sure to generalize, for men or women, alike:

"If you fail, you are unhappy, but if you fail, and everyone else fails, there is a sense of relief".

It was true for a physics paper in 11th grade. When we received grades, everyone was in shock. Nonetheless, when the professor told the entire class marks ranged from "30 to 33" out of 100, which implied everyone had failed, there was a smile all around.

Furthermore, life at the end of high school was categorized into two strata;

"Either you were a geek, or had a pretty face".

But it had left a dent, in my mind, as I fell in neither category - by the standards, or rules set by society. Whether, reel life, or real life, I witnessed,

"All top colleges, needed cent percent marks to get admission, or if you had a pretty face, the glamour industry welcomed you".

Well, that lowered my self-confidence, but did one thing well, as I look back, shut the door of the glamour industry. I opted for education. Despite burning mid-night oil, grades were never like a

bright student, and the reality aligned with the slogan:
"Beauty with a brain, is indeed, a rare combination",
I realized, better to accept myself as mediocre, and be happy, rather than, being constantly unhappy, with the fact, I could have been, at his/her spot. At that moment, I was out, from the rat race, or today, I might say "I changed the course of, the conspiracy".

CHAPTER THREE

BEYOND LINES

College days, atleast, mine were unromantic, in all sense. Probably, it was me, who had set high standards, in all spheres, or it was just, the 21st Century. As everyone said,

"College days, those days, which recollected, later in life, make you either, laugh or cry".

It was days, for me, where I had opportunities, to deploy book knowledge, in reality, to fathom, if everything written in books, were actually true, or not. Whether, it was an infectious disease subject, which emphasized,

"Sterilize petri-dish"

with nothing else, appended post that. As per my experience, it was only possible, in laminar flow, and not on a tabletop, or understanding communication gap, in a department, via reading emails, and why punctuation marks, were pivotal in, the English language, can be understood, by the below sentence:

"Let's eat Grandpa".

"Let's eat, Grandpa".

I went abroad, for my undergraduate so, it was more chaos, as I was adjusting to a new culture, in each and every aspect:

"From understanding their accent, to adopting a new lifestyle, and fitting in their education system".

It was a turnaround, from my own culture, as it taught me, to be independent, contrary, to Indian culture. When I started to work, alongside my education, it was like, losing the comfort of life, and that brought me to "world". However, the world, was yet to be born, as education, took priority.

I applied, for a scholarships. As I look back, I still wonder, if I had met all criteria, yet, did not get one, what could be the reason? Moreover, when I inquired, I was told, "It is for, domestic students", which was a little dubious, as it was opened to international students. Nevertheless, it was the first time, I realized, I might have ignored, reading beyond the lines,

"That one-font size text".

Nevertheless, in the same manner, I ignored this fallacy.

CHAPTER FOUR

TITLE

I worked as a researcher, and there were many chances, to present the work, eventually, what I thought of the country, and their culture, was contradicted by their actions. I won the title, but never received, the gifts, which were supposed to be the prize. But, all I heard, all the time was,

"Congratulations, atleast, you got the title".

The final jolt, was the "Directors" award, and "not the President" award. I was on the verge of receiving, the "President" award, which was the highest recognition, in academics. But, it was snatched away, because of, the 1 mark, in the finals, yeah finale. It is not, that Director's award was worthless, but at the time, I felt unfair, cheated, and that difference of 1 mark, was not a natural, but a deliberate attempt. Again, what I heard was,

"Congratulations, you are getting Director's award, atleast".

Nonetheless, when it came to a job, while everyone preferred, high paying job, because they would not mind, faking their resume, age, experience, and everything on their resume. I selected the one, which aligned with my education, experience, and age. So, definitely, with little experience, or with an accurate number of years of experience, on a resume,

"A job, can't be, high paying".

Again, what I heard,

"Congratulations, you are working as a Scientist, pretty awesome".

According to me, it was not about the award or a job, but it was more like a preference, a fake world. It was not even "a man, and a woman competition - that a man, usually gets, a high paying job", not even "who was better at education", as time and time, my competitors changed, but the outcome remained the same; atleast in education institutions.

I sensed, it was not a destiny, written, that is unfolding, in its natural way, but a hidden conspiracy, or power game. In no time, I realized, it is an attempt, made, again and again, where I was given, the title, but snatched away the prize. Maybe, it was to showcase, how hearing, and doing what power dictates, could buy anything, and everything, and chasing your dream, or being honest, would eventually, make you survive, on paychecks.

CHAPTER FIVE

EDUCATION

In the 21st Century, contrary to the earlier era, where educated people like doctors, scientists, and others made headlines, it was the glamour industry, which began to be more successful, in terms of fame, wealth, and work. The slogan, "beauty without the brain" was not only limited to Page 3, of a newspaper, but it started to peak, even in the workplace, where

"Mind should have been honored, rather than beauty".

It set the stage, that in order to be successful, it is okay, not to be academically good, or be good at writing, but, what mattered was how well, you could hear to power, and speak their language. It was not equally applicable to both genders, but specifically to women. So, a woman, who is apparently good at academics, but inclined to work, rather than hearing to power, was meant to be:

"Out of the workforce, and better be a housewife".

Is it a mirage, or the stage was set to fail women, who were actually the ones working, and were behind the scenes, of successes achieved by men or/and women?

For me, it hinted at educational institutions, but was evident in the workplace, when it came to climbing the ladder.

"In order to get the next promotion,"

What mattered was, how well you were known among authorities, and how well you could hear, and be their slave. Other parameters, work and results, were secondary things to be successful. The amount on the paycheck, was directly linked with your cost of make-up. Seriously?

If you didn't beautify yourself, why did you need a heavy amount, to be paid, when you could live on the current amount? That was the turning point, in my life, and a thought sparked in my mind "Who are leading the world"? Education taught, everything was related to the outcomes, and results, but in practicality, it was related to power.

CHAPTER SIX

MULTIPLE HATS

Multiple hats? People wore multiple hats. Again, a point to ponder, were they only a figure? or had many names? or wearing many masks? If an individual, was actually, "working" or "involved" at a workplace, it was impossible to wear, 9-10 hats, and be equally good at all.

"I found the meaning of multi-tasking".

Well, multiple hats meant, more money. One could have multiple faces, behind which, highly educated, or distressed or needy people were working, while they only be available, at the time of speaking, and taking credits,

"I found the meaning of consulting agency, and was glad, I did not choose that".

So, powerful people, are just lips that speak, rather than a mind, that works. It was a time, when I need to choose AGAIN, between money, and honesty. No doubt, honesty was way cheaper, and meant you would survive, but won't be able to afford luxuries. Apparently, it was obvious, high-priced commodities, were meant for beauties, "multiple hats", not for brain.

A "fake" world, unlike the ancient era, where the Nobel price, was meant, not for NGO workers, but for those, who invented and discovered new things.

"An era of lost wisdom".

I remember, a few professors, who told me, "Whether driving a BMW or Toyota, both did the same thing. Furthermore, there will be times, when you will have to make the choice(s), like the same, and that will decide your future". The only advice they gave, was, "Choose, what makes you happy, as you will have the time, to change it - in case, you want to take, the other turn, and it is only possible, if you are happy and satisfied".

"It was a choice, between, a mind, and lips".

People who spoke, for the work done by others, were looked upon, publicly famous, and had luxurious. At workplace, concepts like

"No free lunch", "Give and take relationship", and "My way or highway" all seem to be true.

However, all these created, a psychological disturbance, that's why, many educated women, quit the workforce, got married, and settled down, rather than, revolting with those, who are leading the world.

CHAPTER SEVEN

LET'S DATE

The biggest trap, was in the word "Date". It had corroded, all other relationships: friendship, brotherhood or sisterhood or brotherhood-and-sisterhood. If two individuals, who were travelling, and roaming together were tagged "they were dating". The world was, either go in a group, or choose to date, as there was no middle way. I was, often, tagged with people, I roamed around. I prefer, company of one, rather than many.

"What does date meant? My journey, to find the truth, began, with this word only."

To date someone, means, to understand the other person, which made sense. But, as it gets deeper, ultimate means marrying. As per ploy, not two, but many means "if you would like to have a fun time, with friends, then why you would not take everyone, with you"? At that moment, it was bitter truth to bite, but rather, than getting tagged, to multiple people, I started to roam alone.

"Then, also, cascade of questions, followed".

What if, you were out late at night, and something happened. I always said,

"Well, I have a phone, and I have police, on speed dial".

It was clear, that society was against, independent women, but then, why it was not written down, in textbooks, and taught in educational institutions.

"The conspiracy whispered, scratch more".

It ignited a tug-of-war, between the two generations, where older ones thought, they were being challenged. But, all I wanted, was freedom to do things, what I wanted, to do, and not follow, society norms, which had tagged, everything with age.

CHAPTER EIGHT

AGE - A NUMBER

Whether, it was during World War I, or World War II, or 21st century, a question, was always raised, for a woman, to choose between "Career" or "Marriage". No matter, how many women, had made to the top, "if they have", in all areas, from business to sports, but the mentality, yet remains the same, "a woman, needs to choose, between the two". Was it a really a woman, needed to choose, or it was society, structured, in such a way, which handicapped, the women, and deprived them, from being "independent".

"The quote, behind every successful man, is a woman."
was actually a false, as it seemed:

"A woman, needs a man, to establish, her career".
The quote, and the truth, when I entered the workforce, left me in a perplexed situation. It was apparent, that education, and the practical world, were not going, hand in hand. If it was so, there had to exist, a structure or path, for everyone, to follow, rather than a question "Career" or Marriage"?

An independent, career-oriented women, meant, one who chooses, to be alone, had no boundaries or responsibilities, and take instinct decisions, without hesitant or consultation. While marriage, for the same woman, meant a barrier, where one had boundaries, and therefore, career took a back seat. It was not a career, or marriage, but apparently, the conspiracy was against, women being independent, or it is just, the way, women of previous generations, wanted, that's why, society was structured, in such a way?

I saw, many of my friends, who married at the age of 23-25, aligning with the society norm, which I was trying to break. When I raised the voice, "why can't one establish, a career from 25 to 35, and then mature enough to decide,

Whether to get married, or not"?

The only answer, I got,

"That is, not the way, society works".

CHAPTER NINE

FREEDOM MATTERS

Career can be molded, changed, or left if it does not work, as it depends on choices made, and likes of an individual. But, getting into a relationship, for life, one needs to understand oneself, first, then choose, atleast, that was taught, to me, from both, religious, as well as personal perspectives. If marriages are like career, then definitely, a reason, why divorce rate, is increasing at alarmingly rate. According to research, in western world, it is nearly 50%, which if translated, mathematically meant:

"Every second person, is divorced",

It is more dangerous, than any plague or pandemic, that prevails in the world. Everyone, can preach about being independent, be successful, make a world better place, and the list, but if individuals in the society, are not mentally or psychologically healthy, due to relationships or career choices, there are no way, society or world, can be a happy place. Though, "in recent times, awareness abour mental health, anxiety, depression, and other psychological illness are increasing, but no one knows, the root cause,

I wonder, if everything tied with age, is the cause".

When I looked around, and talked, I realized, by the information, I gathered, the structure of a woman life follows, the below protocol:

"At 22: Graduation | At 25: Marriage | At 29: Buy a house | At 30: Become Parent | From 30-60: Children and work | At 60: Retirement | From 60 to death: Travel around and wait for death".

I paused, and wondered, what if, I choose to reverse, the order. Many of them, smiled, and said.

"Society will change".

Though, it was complex riddle, but I thought, rather than living, as per society standards or conspiracy, I will take my destiny, in my hand, as I had nothing to lose, and ultimately in both situations "the outcome is either, marriage or death".

It all started, with scratching and cross questioning, on almost everything, listening and acting, as if I wanted to learn. It changed, the way, I looked at things, and saw, how easily people get irritated, if things, were getting cross questioned, and one line, spoken, across by everyone:

"Everyone is following the same thing, things are done like this, stop questioning, and just do what is told".

I often joked "So, you guys married, just because you were 23", and surprising, the answer was, yes. Being a woman, it also added a layer, on how you will get a man, at age of 35, as everyone would be married, you will be left alone, fertility question, and so on. To most questions, I had biological answers, and I only said, if pairs are made in Heaven, one might be left.

CHAPTER TEN

INNOVATION - A MYTH

Does the title sound, contradictory? That is the contradiction, in my life - some did say, it was I, who was overthinking, but again and again, it was not me, it was circumstances, which made the way, I thought. Many people, when graduated, went to a Consultancy agency, and did, some sort of technology role. The beauty of this profile, is it engulfs everyone, from any field of streams, any number of experiences, and any qualification(s).

Computer science, or any field, that directly deals with Computer, are always highly paid, a reason why it boomed, so much, whereas other fields, which invent, discover new things, to make life better, are underpaid, yes underpaid.

"Chase your dream, and money will follow - a myth,".

It was a tough decision, as one get paid, almost triple the amount, that the other paid. I decided that, the path of consultancy, was always open, but try a job, that aligned, directly with the education, that I had received, for almost 7-8 years. One reason, why I did not go for Consultancy, was probably, my disliking toward coding, the technical bent it had, and just thinking on, 0-1 language, binary language.

The less money, killed my desire, to have lavish commodities, but computer science, would have killed my creativity, and probably, it would have been a way, to earn money, than enjoying, what I do. It was not a smooth ride, despite overlooking, money. The job profile was something else, and I was put to work on random things, which did not make sense.

Though, after raising my voice, I was slowly moved to the profile, that I was hired for. But, as dictators, could not tolerate their defeat, they said they were changing the designation, to make it more aligned, with the industry level.

CHAPTER ELEVEN

IF, BUT, WHATSOEVER

If something happened around you, that did not fit as appropriate to you, or anyone else, it was natural human tendency, to speak, and seek answers. But as power corrupts, and as innocent raised their voice, the only thing, which was replied,

"Do you know, who I am?".

At that moment, I realized, one had to gain power by force, to make oneself heard. Additionally, there were scenarios, where even the slightest twist, and turn in their way of doing things, would invite a blazing storm.

"If" was like a jargon, used to tell, "what I shall do", rather than, "freedom to do things". To any question, the best answer, was, "If", I was you, I would have made boyfriend, or got married. I wondered, how that would end the circumstances, or improve it. Why that was a "requirement", to be heard, or able to speak.

"Deep inside I realized, that is the power, dictating the world"

"But" was another word, which had derailed a lot, from its dictionary meaning. Any suggestion, which was bound to favor the listener, was always thought, "but" you know, "I have experience, and I know how things work, and I have reached, to this level, and therefore, it will be done, the way, it is done". It bewildered me sometimes, "are we working to improve things, that was built, or are we going back in times, when human originated from Ape", or:

"We are just aping the things, without using brain, and mind, yes brain and mind".

The last term "Whatsoever", not commonly used, when writing, but apparently it had gained momentum, in older generation. If "experience" folks failed, the work was redirected, and asked,

"Why don't you try the way, you told earlier, and when if you speak, the only term that came from the mouth was, whatsoever".

At that time, I realized the importance of,

"Being calm, and just hear, and speak only when asked, rather than, giving suggestions".

People, who had achieved things by wrong means, are bound to believe, that's the way, therefore, they forced things their way, to hide the truth. Consequently, it indicated their hesitant, to adopt, new ways of doing things, as they lacked experience, and education. Consequently, they failed to understand, why one thought, in a different way.

CHAPTER TWELVE

CRITICISM

For continuous improvement,

 "One needs to listen, to the feedback, one receives, from parents, professors, colleagues, or bosses".

But, the line between feedback, and criticism thins, and when it crosses, it is to show, oneself superior, and other inferior. It was common, when White dominated over Black, or during the period of slavery. Being dusky skin, it was not, atleast, in educational institutions, that racisim had surfaced for me, but slowly, as I started to grow, in workplace, it indirectly, started to surface, especially via feedback on work.

No one is perfect, but when the same piece of work, judged with different opinion, by same person, based on the doer, feedback, often turned, to criticism. It was not, only a way, to degrade someone, but it was a way, to extinguish, the ambition, of an individual desire. It is a way, to say, "It is my way or no way" so,

 "Either follow, or listen to, distasteful comments".

It turned the environment hostile, to work, and eventually takes toll on mental, physical and psychological well-being. At that time, it was quite obvious, that conspiracy was against me shining, and it was conspiring, that I should be behind the scene, and not in front. Being rebellious journey began, at that point, for the same reason,

 "Nothing to lose, and ultimate will be marriage or death".

The thick and opaque strata of society, made it impossible for a newbie, to reach to people, who actually were doers, and let your story be told. The only way, possible was via social media, as there lies no proof of, what was implied, by one's post. Sometimes, the vibe from surrounding was, as if I was the problem, and I always thought,

"If I am the problem, then remove me, and be happy. As I declare, to choose money and power, and willingly to leave, everything for the same".

CHAPTER THIRTEEN

HEALTH IS TRUE WEALTH

If you are healthy, you can turn around, anything. Therefore, it is advised, to focus on health, before working, or running, behind anything, in this world. It is understandable, if you have life, then only, you can do anything, that's a reason why, many sign boards have, "Better late than never". It makes sense, but in present era, it was either,

"You live life, given by power, or speak against, the authority".

It was evident, to me, that the world is being led by dictators, but it made me wonder, if they were actually powerful, or they were hiding themselves, behind those, who were actually working, and getting things done. Slowly, many things, made clear sense, as why, lot of people said, that, you can sell your writing, and make money, as many of thesis, were actually written by, someone else,

"Rather, than the person, who had the name, on it".

The same goes, for almost everything. I remembered, buying "Paracetamol", where pharmacist. just put the code, in the computer system, which reflected the shelve number, and she grabbed it. After she handed it, over to me, and I looked at it, it was, totally a different one. When I countered question, about the accuracy, of the medicine, she said, the computer reflected that. I again said, didn't you read it?

"She turned, to the computer, and said, I will check, and grab the medicine".

I was furious, but kept quiet, and took the medicine. But, at that time, I wonder, for people, who do not have, medical background, or don't understand the language, written by doctors, it was impossible, for them to know, which medicine, they were taking.

"Is it a way, to kill people?"

I kept, this thing to me, but I went to my friends' home, and checked their medicine. One of them said, after having paracetamol, they started to bleed. I grabbed the medication, and read it, it was not paracetamol. I simply said, it is outdated, and grab Crocin, from Walmart, rather than from pharmacist. My doubt, became obvious, and I chose, to boost my self-immunity, than trusting, the doctors or pharmacist. But, was that a way, to harm innocent people, or they were terrorists?

CHAPTER FOURTEEN

Norms Displacement

There are few norms, which are universal, usually, in the form of body language, conveying the same meaning, in all countries, to make oneself, able to communicate, without words. However, to my surprise, society, had changed so much, while textbooks, remained old. It was a reality check, and I understood many people, who often said,

"Corporate differs, from the academic world".

In corporate world, norms differ, from one place to another,

"That's why, the title, Founder, exists, as everything, depends as per their norms ".

They have, ability to set standards, as per their choices, rather than standard, nomenclature. It was bit weird, as handshake, meant a positive gesture, where you acknowledge, or show respect to the person, you shake hands with. However, in some corporate world, it meant, one out of two, had accepted to be,

"Inferior, and will be pressed down, when needed".

Similarly, a lot of things, which were positive indication, had slowly, reversed, in the opposite direction. Smile is a universal language, but in a boardroom, if you smile on some issues, it could backfire, as it could indicate, an inappropriate gesture, especially if genders were opposite.

It was not easy, to grasp everything, and change the mind, which was educated, but slowly, one needs to adopt, and adapt to "new" standards, to survive, or quit corporate world. It was contrary, to concept, which preached about,

"Working with, as it was, working for, which meant, kind of slavery".

Therefore, it hampered innovation, consequently, one prefer, better to start a separate company, rather than changing, the "norms" of the company, as people who had worked for company, for more than a decade, were somehow adjusted, and denied the change.

It became evident that, it was their way, or no way. Feedback, and suggestions, were merely the words on documents, and for records. Agree, with the older folks, which meant to lie indirectly. It was like power questioned, and put the answer, in your mouth, and if one rebels, they need to face hostility. Something. which, made it clear for me, was an incident where,

"Being honest was severely backfired on me".

When in a meeting, someone asked, "so, you are good with the things, and pretty busy". I candidly said, "yeah but could take more". A time, where you made, someone in power, felt "How dare you disagree with me". And the next day, it was bombardment of work, and again, in the next meeting, it was, speaking the language, they wanted, else face the adversity.

It was chaos, which needed to be dissected, to know who were leading the world, and why, few people were being preferred, everywhere, was it a family, which had gained power, and to remain there ,they were willingly to do anything?

CHAPTER FIFTEEN

THE LAST CHALLENGE

It was suffocating, to live ,and even to survive, in the place, that was built by those, who were dictating. I was sure, they would, go beyond anything, if resistance grew against them, but won't kill the person, rather torture them. I had left with two options, go with the flow, or rise against them. Though, it was to jump in a valley, where I did not know, what was there, but made my mind, that rather than succumbing to death, each day,

"I would choose death at once, or will be able to bring, the truth out, either will happen".

When I was about to speak, against the authority, many people said, it was the way, else be ready, to face the consequences. But eventually, it was way to tell them "I am going to do that, hopefully they all know the outcome". After that, as per my thought, hostility and cruelty, became their language. However, with many people, I was indirectly communicating on social media, came in action, which concreted that, my life was safe, and

"I can rebel against anything".

My journey, last challenge, began. Is it me, or a human thing, that, in spite of knowing, that I could go beyond any limit, there was something, inner calling, stopped me, to go to the level, which I saw the power corrupt people went. I choose, to be back at my home country, as working in their environment, was impossible, as they started to realize, that people were listening to me,

"And that their truth was slowly surfacing".

I came back to my home country, and slowly, when people, who too thought, about the hidden conspiracy in the world, slowly started to reveal their own story, and became part of "Shoot Out With The Conspiracy". It was indeed, a family, which framed good people, uses their weakness, as their strengths. To retain the power, they had killed many innocents, and the only way to reach to top was,

"Setting their own rules and regulations, which either make an individual like them, or the individual would, quit or suicide".

As more people joined in, and told the truth, about their life happenings, the power of "hearing" went down, and slowly people in power, started to lose control. Indeed, a family was dictating, and to be in power, they needed to do, what they did with me, or else, their truth would come out. It was power play, and to free myself, from their dictatorship,

"I choose to be a rebel and I defeated death".

No matter who you are, show humility and gratitude, a line spoken by my grandfather, because in a moment of a second, everything can be changed. The mighty force, will guide you to your destiny, brutally or smoothly, but IT will. Power-corrupt people, will drag you down, but trust the Creator, Destroyer and Preserver, to show the path of destiny, else you will be bestowed with Heaven, but not Hell. I succumb, my life, to Goddess ad Gods.

About The Author

Sanjivni, is an accidental writer. She is not a literature, psychology or philosophy graduate. She is a science student, who happened to take a sharp turn, and made her way to business education.

"Shout Out With The Conspiracy", a writing piece, written during the COVID pandemic. It was time, to be at home, as everything, came to stand still, due to viral infection, which was a deadly disease. The narration, in the book, is her own thoughts, and perspectives, on different happenings, which took place in her life. To perceive it as true, it depends on individual experience, and other factors. But, most of the scenarios, written in the book, actually drew from her own life.

Apart from writing, she loves to paint. Since, she had studied, in US and India, her English, is amalgamation of both, British and American, especially, when it comes to spellings. She had travelled, around India and US, and is a strong believer of, First Name.